A New Life

A New Life

All rights reserved. No part of this work covered by the copyright herein may be reproduced or used in any means – graphic, electronic, or mechanical, including copying, recording, taping, or information storage and retrieval systems – without written permission of the publisher.

First published by Griffin Lore, 2024
chris.griffinlore@gmail.com

© Copyright: Chris Griffin

Typesetting and cover design by The Book Typesetters
hello@thebooktypesetters.com
07422 598 168
www.thebooktypesetters.com

The moral right of the author has been asserted.

ISBN 978-1-7394306-2-7

A New Life

Verses for a better world

Chris Griffin

By the same author

A New Attitude
A New Identity

This book is dedicated to all those
who want to live anew in a better world.

Contents

Introduction   9
   *Why do a new attitude and identity not automatically
   guarantee a new life?*

Constantly Growing   11
   Coping with perpetual change as life never stands still.

Making the Right Choices   31
   *The ones that move us unashamedly towards joy and
   happiness…*

Embracing Our Own Metamorphosis   51
   Despite the naysayers and patronisers of this world.

Thriving in the Wider World   73
   Living differently in the well-established Old Order.

Dealing with Our Shadow Side Again and Again…   91
   *Fears never actually go away; we just learn how to deal with
   them.*

From Mind-Led to Heart-Led Lives   109
   From daily fears to happiness and joy each and every day.

So, Where Might All This Take Us?   133
   Or, at least, where is all this taking me?

About the Author	141
Acknowledgements	142
Index	143

Introduction

Why do a new attitude and identity not automatically guarantee a new life?

A new attitude and identity may have been hard-won as you distilled your masculine and feminine. Having faced fears, you may believe that you have tackled the worst and there *is* much to celebrate but… are you ready to openly embody the new you in a world that loves to ridicule non-conformists?

To live a fearless new life is hard, testing your resolve and your belief as you cross paths with others who judge you. You cannot expect them to change or disappear, and hiding away will not give you the full and happy life you deserve. So, what to do?

Hone your skills and your ability to stand firm, content, happy and at peace without being pulled back into fear and chaos. Fine-tune taking your rightful place without justification and without building resentment in others. Show the world that you can live without fear and still be successful, happy and fulfilled. If your life looks so attractive that it piques people's curiosity, others may choose to join you and that is the best way to change the world for the better.

Each of us will sell a new life in our own inimitable way and there is no end to the impressions we can make if we are willing to live anew.

Constantly Growing

Coping with perpetual change as life never stands still.

Going Forwards

I love my life!

It is scary
But wonderful
It is challenging
But rewarding.

It pushes me
It pulls me onwards
No time to hesitate
As life carries me forwards.

If I stop and think
I may start to doubt
To fear
That the worst may happen.

Far better to just
Go with the flow
No time for regrets
And harking back to the past.

What's gone is gone
Whether it was good or bad.
The future though
Is just waiting to happen
Whatever that might be…

A Formula

I can't give you
A formula
To make your decisions easy.
I can point out
Why decisions are hard
But are still worth making
Including those that prove to be
So very, very challenging.

The harder it is to make
The more deeply the power
A decision has
To change
The very fabric of your life.

So, if change is your intention
Don't shirk such decisions
But take your time
And work through them
Till you know
Exactly what feels right.

If things don't just
Fall into place
It is easy to think they are wrong
But maybe they're not…
Perhaps you are being tested
Is your resolve sufficient
To stand the test of time?

Some changes
Will be open to challenge
So you will need to know
How to stand strong
To hold your nerve
And trust that all is well
Even though
It does not appear to be so!

Your intuition
Will tell you what's right
And no formula
Can ever replace
The accuracy
And pure creativity
Of our precious
And far-seeing intuition!

Losing Control

The status quo cannot be maintained
However much we may want to stay there!
We may fight the flow
Keep hanging on by our fingertips
Becoming more and more stressed
As the momentum builds up
Like a dam ready to burst
At any moment.

Letting go is a relief
When all's said and done
With our direst imaginings
Failing to materialise.

It is, though, scary as we have to relearn
How to stay agile
And how to go with the flow
As we get used to not being in control
As we let fate or destiny
(Or whatever you choose to call it)
Take over our lives.

The one overriding factor though
Is that the struggle eases
As we stop trying to hold back the tide.

Right up to the End

The past
Is not the measure of your life.
It is only at the end of your life
When all the twists and turns
Have taken place
And you have evolved
Into a final version of you
Just before life ends…
Only then can the full extent
Of your life be measured.

Change is possible
At any time
Right up to the end.
Allow it to happen
By not in any way
Prejudging the outcome.

Must I Really?

When you finally
Let go
Of that which you believed
Would be yours forever
Then your life
Can really, truly
Start afresh.

No ties.
Complete freedom
To be yourself
In your unimaginably
True magnificence!

It is only then
That you discover
That it is absolutely worth
The ultimate letting go.

The Meaning of Safe

Safe.
What does that mean to you?
Safe to let go, to be yourself
To reflect deeply
About what really matters to you.
Or safe only in the material sense
Which often requires continual work
No time to reflect and assess
Whether you are really happy
Whether you are really content.

As the former requires a focus
Away from the material
And towards introspection
The daily whirl that we have today
Allows so little space for it to happen.
So, the question is…
Are we the poorer for that?

Persuaded

How another lives their life
Is not for you to decide.
How another might try
To influence
How you might live your life
Is, though, another matter.

Do not be persuaded
Or even swayed
To act against
Your best interests.

You might choose though
To be persuaded
If indeed you feel so inclined
And when your interests are not at risk.
Particularly
If you discover such changes
Will quite likely enhance your life.
Then and only then
Those changes might very well
Be worthy of consideration.

But never be persuaded
To effectively limit yourself.
It might seem in the short term
To be beneficial
But in time
Can lead only to regret.

So, discernment is required
With a view to the long term
And where you are going in your life
And that is something
Only you can know.

So never rely
On another to know
What serves you best
In the life *you* are living.

Evolving

When did we lose our respect for age?
When did we start to idolise youth?
At what point did we start to deny the inevitable
To strive to hold back the tide?

Life is about change
About moving on
About seeing the value in life each day.
If it gets harder to see any value
Perhaps it is progression
That we are fearing
As we are being pushed
Outside of our comfort zone
Rather than standing still.

So is it change
That is making us fearful
As it takes us into uncharted territory?
Perhaps we feel unable to cope
With changes that seem
To be outside of our control.
No, better to hold onto what we are used to
To stunt our lives, to hold time at bay.
But put like that it does make clear
The fantasy of such desires.

No one ever claimed life was easy
And maybe that is because
It requires us to feel comfortable
With inevitable change
So that we as a person do not standstill
So that we as a person keep evolving.

Breathe

Just stop
Just be
Let serenity in.

Calm those roiling thoughts
That go round and round
Inside your head
Building pressure and triggering fears.

Breathe…
Slow everything down
Empty your mind for a moment
Be open
To seeing things differently.

See your fears
As being conjured up
By your mind
Worst case scenarios
Happening all at once.
They are though
A fantasy of the future
A future which does not concern you
Right here and now.
A future that
More often than not
Will never come to pass.

So… breathe…
Enjoy this moment…
Let yourself be happy
For this moment…
And let the future
Simply unfold as it will
Without such fearful anticipation.

Mind-Boggling

Intuitively you know what to do
But the mind boggles
At the thought.

It fears, it doubts
It sounds
Like the sane voice of reason
But it is only stopping you
From spreading your wings
And taking flight
Into a brand-new
And far more exciting world
Which may test you
Expand you
Push you forwards
On to far, far greater things…

The Devil You Know

We say:
'Better the devil you know than the devil you don't'
On the one hand, logical, rational, common sense
On the other, a sure-fire way to ensure continuity
Of the existing discomfort, the less than ideal.
Stagnation.
If such is the best-case scenario, it begs the question:
How do we change the devil
If we don't take a risk on the devil we don't know?
A devil that perhaps isn't even a devil!

So, is the devil you know really the better option
Or is it just the argument of a fearful mind?
A mind that simply fears change
A mind intent only on running away
With dire imaginings
Just dire enough to keep you… well… stuck.

'There'

We never get 'there'
There is no 'there' to get!
We just keep living in the moment
Doing what feels right
As we evolve and change
Throughout our lives.

We may surprise ourselves
When we end up
Somewhere we never expected to be.
When we end up achieving
What we used to believe
Would be impossible to do.

So, never limit yourself
By making plans
That have a specific destination.
Rather
Be flexible
And go where life goes…
However scary and testing
It might become.

But then
Perhaps that's precisely how
We end up achieving
The totally unexpected.

Making the Right Choices

The ones that move us unashamedly towards joy and happiness...

Heart Truths

Your heart cannot be deceived.
You can though
Choose to ignore its truths
Particularly if they're inconvenient.

When your mind
Is full of wishful thinking
Then it really does not matter
Whatever it is that your heart knows…
And that is when mistakes are made
Because discernment
Is no longer at play.

You ignore your heart at your peril
As remorse will come along
Sooner or later.

But your heart is constant
And will always be there
To guide you afresh
However far you have found yourself
To have drifted in the past.

You just need to be
Willing to properly listen
This time around.

Ours

We are the authors
Of our own destiny
Whether we like it or not!
We are the sum of
The decisions and choices
We have made
Throughout our lives.

Those decisions and choices
Will have been governed by
Our beliefs
Our fears
Our doubts
Our shame
And you will note
There is a common word
In all of the above…

This is a double-edged sword
As it clearly indicates
That it is ours but ours alone
To sort out.

So if we really want to make
Much better choices and decisions
We must take a deep breath
And then move one step at a time.
It is a process
That promises us
A very much happier future.

TINA

We believe
'There Is No Alternative'
An alternative that could be better.
We see the flaws
But however hard we think
No better version springs to mind.
We put up with the niggles
We get on with life
Wishing it could be better.

Then suddenly we see the solution
Why didn't we think of it before!
Well perhaps the problem
Was that by engaging the mind
We unknowingly limited our options!

When solutions suddenly spring into our heads
Our minds are not the source.
It is our intuition
That solves the conundrum
And often very simply at that!

What a shame intuition is so low
On the scale that we use
Of what it is
That will make our lives successful.

If we make space
To silence our minds for a moment
So our intuition can come to the fore
We may be surprised
At how alternatives broaden
And solutions just come our way!

Easily Done

It is so easy
To be completely unaware
When it is fear that governs
Our decisions.

We limit our lives
By expecting the worst
And then we wonder
Why it is that our lives
Remain so very limited…

We dream of the best
But plan for the worst.
Which might explain a lot!

Listening to Our Hearts

My heart speaks to your heart.
But if you have stopped
Listening to your heart
We have no common language.
We remain aloof and distant
No meeting of minds even
To fill the void.

So, is this the end of us?
Yes, with no change
I suspect it is.
And whether that is
The right or the wrong way to go
It would require us both to listen to our hearts
And not to our minds instead.

Pandering

What motivates us
To do what we do?
It is important to know
To work it out.

So often when we do good things
It is why we are doing those things
That matters.
Because we genuinely want to
Or because we really need to?
The first makes those good things good
The second questions their validity.

Are we doing something good
To keep someone onside
To point-score
To burnish our reputation?
These motivations
We are likely to hide
From others
And especially from ourselves.

No.
We want to bask in the glory
Of being seen to be doing good
Or we need to bolster
Our position
When we feel at risk of losing something.

Instead of focusing
On what it is
We give to or do for others
We would benefit more
By turning our gaze
On our own ulterior motives.
We need to ask why
We have to pander to such motives
Which is then of course
The reason why
We end up pandering to others.

More Than Enough

When we have more than enough
Do we rejoice in our comfort?
Do we share and give
Without fear of loss?
Do we actually feel secure and contented?

Or do we fear that we might lose our wealth
Do we feel it is never enough?
Do we tailor our lives
To hold on to what we possess
Dreading that it might
Be taken from us?

Are our decisions driven
By defensive actions
To safeguard
All that we have got used to?
If that is the case
The overriding principle
Then contentment will stay
Way out of our reach.

We may gain or lose in life
Such is our reality.
It is how we deal with
Both the gains and the losses
That makes our lives
Either happy or fearful.

If I Were You...

If I were you…
A phrase that precedes
Some form of advice
Intended to help you out.

But no one is you
Except for you
So the premise
Upon which the advice is based
Is baseless and therefore
Quite lacking authority.

So give yourself permission
To turn a deaf ear
On those misguided
Good Samaritans.

Only you are the judge
Of what's best for you
So believe in yourself
And what feels right.
Then be brave
And act on your
Own inner guidance.

The Line

We toe the line
We dare not cross it.
We sacrifice our own authenticity
To stay on the right side of the line.
But who decides
Which is the right side?

If we dare to cross it
We soon discover
Who has decided what is right.
We are deemed
To have put a foot wrong
To have stepped out of line
The line that cannot be seen
But can be felt
So very, very deeply.

A line that divides
Approval from disapproval.
A line that causes so many of us
To people-please
And so sell our souls
To gain approval…

What a price it is
That we choose to pay
If we do not muster the courage
To cross that line.

Right or Wrong?

In answer to the question
'What is your *raison d'être*?'
How many of us say
'To be happy'?

How many of us are too focused
On what we are meant to do
Instead of how we feel
About what it is we are doing?

What makes us happy
Is what we should do.
Though many of us
Might think this too trite.

But as we strive to succeed
At some grand plan
We might stop and reflect
Is it making us happy?

And if we are not
Do we then stop and ponder
Perhaps that's because
We haven't yet found
The right *raison d'être* for us?

If Truth Were Told

Quit doing
What others tell you
Is the right thing to do.

Start doing
What feels right
What makes *you* happy
What brings *you* joy.

Deep down you know
What is right for you
So, you will know the difference
If you make the time
To stop and listen
To your heart.

The choice is yours
Keep others happy
Or
Keep happy yourself.
Put like that
It sounds so simple…

But many of us
Know that it's not
As we must get over
The urge to people-please
Without feeling guilty
And worrying that we are
Being selfish.

So, my advice is
Dig deep into why
We need to please others
Rather than please ourselves.

It is self-sabotage
When all's said and done
And few will thank you
For doing that.
Eventually
Not even yourself
If truth were told!

Disruption

For change to occur
There must be disruption of the status quo.
But care must be taken
To differentiate between
Disruption of the status quo that results in change
And disruption only of the process of change.
The latter being more intent
On sustaining the Old Order
The old status quo.

In times of change like now
Those who embrace the role of disruptor
Should be open to others
Questioning their motives.

Embracing Our Own Metamorphosis

Despite the naysayers and patronisers of this world.

Who Are We?

We are who we are
There is no judgement necessary.
So many of us twist and distort ourselves
To please others, to meet expectations
To conform.

Such roles chafe us day in, day out.
They torment us in the dark of night.
We dress in the morning
Not noticing how we put on our roles
As well as our robes.

In time, we forget who we are.
When we undress
We fail to remove that layer, our role, our mask.
It has so firmly stuck to our skin
That we mistake it for who we truly are.

Some of us live our whole lives
As a being alien to our true selves.

The lucky ones of us sense our self-deception
And start along the painful path
Of peeling away hard-stuck layers
Exposing the wonderful, vibrant being
That has been hidden from sight all along.

An Image

It may come as a bit of a shock
When you realise
You are not who you thought you were!

When you are not
Your image
Your appearance
Your set of beliefs
Your behaviours
When all of those
Are actually quite alien to you!

Why couldn't you see
How you were deluding yourself
By trying to be
An image
A role
A good person?
That is, of course, good
In the eyes of others!

When you see through
The illusion
That is just the beginning
As you start to find out
Who you really are
Having ignored yourself
For so very long.

So, if you don't already know for sure
Who you really are
How do you know
The old you isn't you?
Which is a very good question
You might ask!

It all boils down to feelings in the end
And even that is difficult
If you have learnt
To ignore those feelings
Over many, many years
In order to be the old you!

So, if you really want
To ask that question:
Am I me or just an image?
Be honest and dig up
Those perhaps long-buried feelings…

Are you happy?
Are you content?
Do you feel joy every day?
Are you at peace
In whatever you do?
Do you simply feel 'just right'?

You will know the answer
If you take time to reflect.

So, are you real
Or just an image?

Do not be fearful
If you are not real.
No.
Pat yourself on the back
For being brave enough
To see through
The illusion
And beyond
Into the glorious
But as yet
A little bit scary unknown you.

Beauty

When the surface allure fades
You can no longer rely on
The superficiality of youth.
You must find what endures within you
Your real, deep-seated attraction
The attraction that does not fade
But lives on and grows with age.

Confidence in self
Knowing and exuding
Your real strengths and natural beauty
Is far more attractive
Than promoting the artificiality of youth.

It is the unique you
And cannot be duplicated by any other.
It mimics and copies no one
It is you, undiluted and untarnished
And it lasts a whole lifetime.

All Rolled up Into One

Many do not understand
Their feminine side
Or any feminine, full stop.
If truth were told!

They try to understand
To rationalise
To describe
And so predict and control
The way the feminine works.

No wonder the feminine
Gets such bad press
In the hands of those
Who do not understand!

And they will never understand
Unless they first understand
One very important thing…
A feminine
Both their own and everyone else's
Can only be accessed
Through their feelings
For which
Acknowledging and owning emotions
Is an essential prerequisite.

For a feminine is irrational
Unpredictable
Uncontrollable
And ultimately
Indescribable in words!

So, there's the solution
And ultimately the very big problem
All rolled up into one!

Naysayers

We have a new word 'delulu'
And it is a word that easily triggers
The naysayers of this world.
Those who eagerly grasp it to add
To their particular list of reproofs.

But what if such reproofs
Shine the light upon them
Rather than their intended focus?

'They use it in jest'
Might be the retort
'To have a bit of fun.'
But fun which intends
To discomfort others
Is not really intended to be much fun.

Perhaps using delulu
In a pejorative way
Is because that person
Just feels quite envious
Because their beliefs
Do not allow them to imagine
Such a wild and wonderful future!
So let's puncture the hopefulness
Of those who do imagine
So they can be miserable too!

What spoilsports they are!
And furthermore
How do they know
The future any better
Than those who are delulu?

It is their beliefs
That limit views of their future.
But then they so smugly believe
That their view
Of a limited future
Must, by necessity, apply to all.

They are quite free to go on living
Their own self-limited lives.
But I ask they desist
From insisting that others
Share in their joylessness too!

Pep Talk

Our own conditioning
Will resist big change
The need to admit
We might have
To do better.
Our enthusiasm
Wavers
When we don't get
The desired outcome
As easily as we thought we would.

Perhaps we are wrong
To keep ploughing this furrow
Is a question
That gets louder and louder.

But to give up feels wrong
Despite being
The oh-so sensible option.
So perhaps it's just hard
And is not in fact wrong…

Perhaps what's attempted
Is bound to be tough
And so it's determination
That is called for…

Keep going, keep going
For as long as it takes
And so long as it feels it is right.

Because…
Of course it is hard
Or it would have
Happened already.
In your heart you know
That that is so.

So keep going
You *will* find others who get it
And are willing to stand alongside
To add their voice to the message
Until the volume
Can be heard by all.

What drives us forward
Is instinct
Not logic.
So when in despair
It serves us
To always remember that.

If it's hard
(And big change is)
Then expect despair
To come knocking at the door.

Be prepared for a rough ride
Hang on, don't give in
That change is so worth
Rising to the challenge
However hard that may be!

(I needed this pep talk
And so too may you!)

Be It!

Be it.
You don't need
To talk about it
Explain it
Or justify it.

Just be it
Put it out there
As a way of life
That brings you
Contentment and happiness.

Let others reach
Their own conclusions
As it doesn't matter
What they decide
Because it doesn't change
How you might choose
To go on living your life.

And if they decide to join you…
Great!
Because you will no doubt find
That 'the more the merrier'
Is more than just a saying!

Spotlight

Are you in the spotlight
Or are you the spotlight
Shining a light
On what needs to change
For the world
To be fairer to all?

Either way
You may garner attention.
Are you ready for that?
Because that's what makes you strong.

Rejects and Misfits

When is a reject not a reject?
When is a misfit not a misfit?
When they don't fit a narrative
Or set of circumstances
But fit other narratives
Or circumstances perfectly.

So, perhaps it's the narrative
Or circumstances
That really need to change
Rather than requiring
The so-called rejects or misfits
To be a necessary sacrifice.

Knowing

Intuitive knowing was called witchery
Because of the lack of empirical evidence
Something unsupported by logic and reason
So deemed fanciful
And even, at times, downright dangerous!

So what is a feminine supposed to do
If to reveal intuitive skills
Risks being branded a witch or something similar?
Well, to embrace being a witch
Is one very powerful option
To cast light on the falsity of the myths and the legends
That have endured for far too long
Resulting in the silencing of feminine intuition
The knowing that so scares
The ever so fearful rational mind.

My Way...

'My way or the highway'
Will be an oft repeated requirement
By some others in your life
Until you choose
To stand your ground.

Until you stand strong enough
To make such requirements
Completely irrelevant to your life
So they just bounce
Straight off you
With barely a glancing blow.

Those 'my way-ers'
Will grow hoarse
Trying to make themselves heard
At least by those
Who have learnt
To stand strong.

Damaged Ego

Observing and witnessing
Damaged ego at play
Becoming aware of its nature.
Acknowledging it
And then letting it go
So it no longer exerts any power.

Thriving in the Wider World

Living differently in the well-established Old Order.

Bamboozled

Do not be bamboozled
By the material world.
It limits and clouds
Our vision
And makes our lives
All the poorer for that!

Boundaries or Barriers?

If your boundaries are weak
You'll find yourself
Building strong barriers
To keep ill-wishers at bay.

If your boundaries are strong
(Meaning you exercise discernment)
You do not need
Any barriers
As ill-wishers
Cannot even get close.

Barriers keep everyone at bay.
They also conceal you
From the world.

Strong boundaries
Are therefore required
If you are to meet
All those wonderful people
Who have your best interests
At heart.

Living Space

Making space
For a new way of living
Is not easy.

I'm not talking about
Living differently
Behind closed doors
Hidden away from sight.

I'm talking about
Living in a new way
In plain sight
As part of the mainstream
Despite the ridicule
And the pressures to conform.

But
Without such bravery
To live anew in full view
We are destined
To live a lie
At least
For a large part of our lives.

Contagion

Fear is contagious.
So how to buffer yourself
From the fear of others?
How to stop yourself
Succumbing?
How to live
A parallel, fearless life
Yet still remain wholly visible
To all in the world
And keep playing your part too?
How to venture out
From your safe space
And still maintain your integrity?

All of this
Is not an easy task.
It takes lots of practice.
There are no short cuts
No avoiding
The conflict created
By such a gulf
Between very differing world views.

There are no ready-made solutions
And we are all required
To work it out for ourselves
In a way that suits ourselves.

It may seem as if
You are muddling along
And it certainly can get very messy.
But don't give up
Or fear you are missing a trick.
Don't think it is too hard…

Instead, celebrate
Even the tiniest progress
As you learn to hold your own
And remain serene
In such a sea of anguish.

I Don't Know

It's fine not to know.
In fact, as none of us
Knows the future
In all honesty
No one knows!

Others may think they know
Because they have plans
Ambitions, goals
And the determination and drive
To achieve them.
But even they
Can't guarantee
That all will actually go to plan…

So, don't worry
If you really don't know
Where you are going
Or what should be coming next.

Expect inner turmoil
As best will in the world
Does not make not knowing
Any easier!
Which is why so many
Make detailed plans
To kid themselves
They are really in control.

But unrealised plans
Lead to great disappointment
And facing the prospect
Of failure!
No concrete plans
Swerves that dilemma
Which is a very big plus!

So what to do?
Simply be ready…
Be aware of the signs
And follow where life leads.
Do not be ashamed
Of speaking a truth:
That you do not know
Your destination.

As I have already said
No one knows
Their actual destination
But many will not thank you
For pointing that out
As if you should doubt
Their plans and commitment!

Mini-Men

This verse unusually
Refers to men and women.
Why do men who say
They both respect and admire
The women in their life
Only really respect
Those who do in fact
Act sufficiently like
Mini-men?

'Oh no they don't!'
Might be the retort
They want their women
To be women
And they are genuine
In their affections!

But please look closer…
Are their women
Trusted when using their intuition
Their knowing with no evidence?
Or are they expected
To be rational and logical
In order to be believed?

Are they required
To fight and compete
To gain plaudits and reward?

Are they allowed
To show their emotions
Without being ridiculed?

Are they allowed
To prioritise
Caring work
Of either young or old
Without being at risk
Of being devalued
And even dismissed
As having
Wasted their full potential?

In short
Are they found wanting
For bravely acting as someone
Who is not a mini-man?!

Beyond the Consensus

It is hard
Stepping beyond
The consensus.
It is easier
To agree or stay silent
So keeping
The spotlight off you.

When you are ready
To stand firm
In your convictions
Only then are you ready
To stand in the spotlight.
And it is that spotlight
That makes it so difficult
Because it is impossible
To avoid it.

Believers

It is those who believe
(I will call them Believers)
That they are doing good
From their own singular point of view
Who are so very, very difficult to deal with
By anyone having any alternative point of view
And for whom the Believers'
Version of good just doesn't work.

Believers may feel aggrieved that
Their goodness is being questioned.
They may feel like a victim
Of those who are less good.
And by less good I mean
Less good in the Believers' eyes.

A Believer needs to be doing good
So to have such goodness questioned
Is anathema to their ears.
And this must be borne in mind
When you do not share their beliefs
To the point that you are compelled
To have to do something about it.

P.S. And remember
Others may find you to be a Believer too
And so treat you accordingly.

Gaining or Losing?

We are in touch with
More and more people
But in less and less
Personal ways.
Acquaintances proliferate
Often at the expense of our friends.

Is this the way
We really want to go
If it is friends who support us
And make life a joy?
Might we be losing
Rather more than we're gaining?
It might be worth pondering on that.

Focus

We believe we must
Be doing something
In order to be successful
In order to achieve.
But maybe we just need
To be something.

It is the being
Not the doing
That is important.

It is our focus
That leads us astray
That leads us
To doing not being.

The doing is simply distraction
From the far more rewarding
Being.

Pyrrhic Victory

Leave behind
Drama and chaos!
Those things that exhaust us
Drain us
Wring us out
And leave us empty-headed
As we seek to recover.

Let all of that
Go over your head.
Find the still, calm
Deeper depths
Unperturbed
By the fast eddies and flows
Of a life too hectic
To be rewarding.

Do not be ashamed
For opting out.
Your life will be richer
When all's said and done
Because
You did not trade
Too much of yourself
In order to win
A pyrrhic victory.

Success!

How do you measure success?
Assets, possessions
Money in the bank
Investment portfolios
In short, tangible assets
Those that can be seen
And counted?

If so
Will you ever have enough of those
Or does having them
Only generate a need for more
Amid a fear that they might be lost?

That sort of success
Risks being
All-consuming
Swallowing up our lives
Till nothing is left
For anything other than
Amassing and safeguarding
A fortune…
And where is the freedom in that?

Dealing with Our Shadow Side Again and Again...

Fears never actually go away; we just learn how to deal with them.

House Room

What if all those things
We don't want
That seem to follow us around
Only do so
Because we give them house room?

We allow them to remain close
While claiming we don't.
They are buried so deep
So part of what's familiar
That to let them go
Feels virtually impossible to do …

We might not like them
But we can't do without them
How bizarre is that!
They might not do us any favours
But we still can't let them go.

Until we recognise
Our own role in them
Hanging around
Like unwelcome guests
They will continue to do so.
Are you prepared for that?

Fearless

If you say that you are fearless
Then you do not know yourself!

You are fearful of even admitting
That you too are not perfect, that you too have fears
That you too are human.

A fear lies in places you care not to look.
A fear lies in what you choose to ignore
The things you won't engage in.
The things, you believe,
Are never going to be for you.

You may be a physical risk-taker
Envied by those who wish they were like you
Brave, so adventurous, so willing to 'go there'
So how could you possibly be fearful?
Dig deeper.
Search harder.
You've buried it deep.
What is it you cannot admit to?
Why the bravado?
What is it you're hiding?
You do know what it is
However busy you keep yourself.

To be at peace and fully content
You must lift the lid on that fear.
To be vulnerable enough to know all of you
The you that is both good
And bad, so to speak.

In short, admit to yourself
That you too are human
And that you, like everyone else
Is completely imperfectly perfect.

Rationing

Fearful people
Are mean-spirited
In some way or another.

They fear losing something
Or of not having enough
Of something
And strictly ration
That something
Or even exclude it
From their lives
So later loss
May be prevented.

And so inadvertently
They blight their lives
By being mean-spirited
Because of their fears.

Shadow Side

You will constantly meet up
With your shadow side.
You think you've got it licked
Have put it to bed
Allowing you to just get on
With the easier things in life.

Then up it pops again
To taunt you and to trip you up
Just when you thought it was safe!

Do not worry.
This is not about your inadequacy.
It is all about making you stronger
To the point that you can take
Your shadow side
Completely in your stride.

It never goes away
But it can cease
To confound or bother you
As you learn to accept it
As a part of you
The you that is unique.

Belief

Profound, unshakeable belief
Drives all those
Who succeed in achieving
Their dreams
Through seemingly impossible feats.

Which begs the question
Why do we think
That our dreams
And the feats required
Will prove to be beyond us?

Why do we doubt?
Why do we expect
Only to be defeated?

It is those answers
That hold us back
And stop us
From making the impossible
Possible…

Fallible

In your heart
You know what is right.
It is your mind
That complicates things
That questions
And doubts
And introduces so many fears.
It is that
That stops you
Simply following your heart …

So now you know
The answer should be simple!
But how to switch off
Your so persistent mind?

That's the test
And it takes lots of practice.
So don't think you are failing
If you struggle to do it.

You are
Like everyone else
Quite fallible
So the real test is not to give up.

First Love

Memories of a first love
Endure because of their intensity.
If such a love is not lasting
How hard it is
To reproduce those feelings
With another.

What if that is because
We have lost our naivety
Our openness to feelings
Our trust in those feelings?

What if, to experience
Such intense wonder again
We must drop our guard
Our protective barriers
All those legacies
Created from the demise of our first love?

What if, for love to bloom again
Wonderfully, gloriously
We must become
As trusting and open as a child
Just like we were
The first time around?

If that is the case
No wonder so many of us
Fail to find
A more than good enough replacement
For that joyous
So clearly remembered first love.

Busy, Busy

The world
Keeps us busy
With its vast array
Of choices within our grasp.
Our lives
Keep us busy
As we make our choices
From such a vast array.
Be it family or work
Or so-called
Leisure activities
Where leisure is not the point!

But our busyness
Has a downside
Whatever the source
As we lose sight of ourselves.
With no time
For pausing and reflecting
On how we and our bodies
Are coping with our busyness.

Are the choices we make
Coming from our heart
Or from a need to be needed
Or a need to be seen
To be doing
Whatever it is we are doing?

Are we even able to stop…
To really reflect
To really assess
To really feel
Just what it is…
That makes us feel on top of the world
Content and at peace?

Or do we feel guilt
That we are not pulling our weight
Not taking enough care of others
At risk of not being seen
As good
Or great
Or in charge
Or powerful
Or whatever else is so important
That it overrides
Whether it's actually doing us any good

The answer to that
May trigger denial
Which is a clue that all is not well
From our own point of view

The point of view
When other's needs and opinions
Are not the most essential
Part of the equation.

Unfathomable

Dealing with the unfathomable
How hard is that!
The mind craves and
Absolutely requires understanding.
It fears living with the unknown
The unknowable.

What arrogance it is to think
That our minds can get to the bottom
Of how the world works
In this vast limitless cosmos.
There is no bottom
To reach
It is unfathomable.

So peace is not gained
By understanding
And controlling.
It is gained by trusting
And believing
That all is well.

Selective or Equal?

We wish to be selective
About who is deserving
And who is not.

But if we are all equal
Does that mean
We are therefore
All equally deserving
Whatever we might have done?

And if that is so
How might that
Scramble our brains
And test our truths
To the point of destruction?

It certainly
Scrambles mine!

Banishment

I fear letting others
Into my life.
I fear being controlled
Being subsumed
Losing myself in the process.

Perhaps my fear
Is really about
My ability to say no.
My ability to put myself first
To not be ashamed
Of who I am.
In short
I fear I am not up to
Standing up for myself…

Which of course
Is ridiculous!
Because it is only me
Who feels those fears
And therefore
It is completely up to me
To bite the bullet
And banish them
Entirely from my life!

Illusions

Ignoring the blindingly obvious
Making excuses for the inexcusable
Wanting to see only the best
In those you care about.
Turning a deaf ear
On others who can see
Through your
Quite false illusions.

In time it will become
Blindingly clear
How you have duped yourself.
But do not feel ashamed
That you were so easily fooled
Because it happens
To many, many people
Who, like you
Choose to hide their own
Self-assessed stupidity.

Far better to see
The progress you've made
In acknowledging your own illusions.
Then consign it all
To the annals of history
And set forth on
A far better future.

From Mind-Led to Heart-Led Lives

From daily fears to happiness and joy each and every day.

Wildest Dreams

On no you can't!
Impossible!
Don't be silly!
Do you want
To be seen as a fool
A mad person?
Someone who's completely
Lost the plot
Too woo-woo to be credible!
Too— SLAM, click…

Just slam and lock
The lid on all those
Mind-based fears
So you can
Live your new life in peace.
Then even your wildest dreams
Can come to fruition.

Big, Small or Infinitesimal

We talk about equity
Being something worth achieving
But what might that really mean
In practice?

Imagine a world
That is truly equitable…
Where your opinion
Your value
Your impact on others
Is exactly the same
As everyone else's
Without having to change who you are to fit in!

Spend just one day with that imagining…
What changes would need to take place
In order to fit that new brief?
Those changes
Might not just be external
As the concept
Might start to scramble *your* brain!

At the end of the day
Reflect on what you have learned
In order to see
How profoundly
The world could change
If indeed
Everyone was truly equitable…

Then reflect some more
About what you can do
To help redress the balance.
It might be big, it might be small
It might even be infinitesimal.
But if everyone does
Even the smallest of things
It can start to mount up
To much bigger change.

So, do not lose hope
Do not stay stuck in a rut
Find something to do
That makes you feel more equitable.
Your life will be better for that.

Love Is the Key!

How can I say
Love is the key to happiness
When speaking
To a loveless, fearful world?

Where love of self
Has been battered and bruised
By experiences of
Fear, doubt and guilt.

And where love of self is absent
So too
Is real love for others.
Pure love
Not co-dependence
Or lust or entitlement
But unconditional love
Straight from the heart.

So step one
Is love of self
Best achieved by looking at
Our own fears, guilts and doubts.
If those remain
We will find ourselves
Judging others
So that we ourselves
Can feel better.

It is those judgements
That lead on
To wars and hatreds
That are so engrained
And so enduring.

So, yes, love is the key
Specifically
Love of self first.
Well, that's easy…
Isn't it…?

Parallel World

The Old Order will not let go
Of their ruling status.
Why would they
When any change
Would be so detrimental
When looking only through their eyes?
No one can blame them
For standing up for themselves
Even though others may suffer.

As their defensive action ramps up
It helps to understand
That it is when one feels cornered
One lashes out the most.

So, when hoping for change
Being too strident
Too forceful
Too aggressive
Will spectacularly backfire
And succeed only in burning more bridges
Than building any new consensus.

What's left
Is the question
If change is to be achieved.

Slow and steady.
Belief in yourself.
Looking for opportunities
To make your alternative mark
To build a parallel more forgiving world
That makes the Old Order irrelevant.

To build your world despite
Whatever others may say
So you can offer it as an alternative.
Then let others make their own choices
To live in your world
Or to remain in the old one.

But remember don't make your new world
Too rarefied and too inaccessible
If you want to make it desirable.
Not everyone will be ready
To make such significant big leaps.

Slow and steady are the watch words
With small steps along the way.
Have an aim in mind
But be ready to adapt
When intuition tells you it's necessary.

Jigsaw

We all have pieces
Of a big jigsaw puzzle.
No one has more than their piece.

It is only when pieces
Are slotted together
That a glimpse
Is seen of the possible picture.

That is why
We are all so different
And why those differences
Are so essential
And therefore should be respected
As is collaboration
And a coming together
If big change
Is to be on the cards.

Inconvenient Truth

What is an inconvenient truth?
It is something that does not fit the narrative
That upsets the Order
That hints at chaos
But that nevertheless
Insists on persisting.

How to deal with it
When it won't go away?
Let's call it an anomaly
An outlier
An aberration
An exception that proves the rule
Anything but acknowledge
Its veracity
Its existence
As being something
That might be of note!

But what if it indicates
A more significant truth
That the narrative needs to be changed
That the world as we know it
Might not really exist
That what we believe to be true
Is far too simplistic
And that our minds have failed to grasp
The true complexity of the world?

Unconditional Love

It's all about love!

Such views trigger the response
Oh! Don't be so naive
That's fantasy, Cloud Cuckoo Land
It won't work in the real world.
Toughen up, grow up
Get real.

But what if it *is*
All about love?
Unconditional love
Of all our fellow human beings.
Not the fairy-tale
Romanticised
Hero-saving heroine
Type of love.

Unconditional love
Is hard to give.
It is also hard to receive.
Nothing soft and fluffy about it.
It tests us to destruction
Often literally
As wars may be triggered
If it cannot be achieved…
And so very often it can't
More often than not in fact.

So when I say
It is all about love
I am not being sentimental
I am setting out a challenge
To each and every one of us.
A challenge that can take
A lifetime to achieve
And even then, may miss
The full mark.

And when I say
It's all about love
Please don't dismiss me
As being
Just a lightweight
A fantasist
Who has yet to learn about life.
It is because
I have learnt so much about life
That I am able to say
That really it is all about love.
Or, unfortunately
The all-too-frequent
Absence of love.

A Much Better World

As a person will only change
When they personally
Can see a need for change
You will need to demonstrate an alternative
That is attractive enough
For another to want to join you...
And another and another...

Until a tipping point is reached without force
And the world changes...

So, exude your contentment!
Be the change you want to see.

You do not need to know
How to change the world
Just keep living your new life.
It is energy that changes
And influences the world
Not plans or schemes.
Set an intention
And live each moment accordingly.

Gently, persistently
Show another way of living.
It reasons with others
It does not force
But it does not capitulate either.

Embody change
Live in the flow moment by moment
Recognising fears when they arise
And managing them
Remaining truly happy and content
While juggling the discords of this world
Living by example day by day
Like forging a new path
Smoother and less arduous.

Not hiding away
Becoming a hermit
Concealing your new life.
No one learns from that.
No one sees how it could work for them.
How possible it is to coexist
Without compromising yourself
And without being cowed into capitulation.

What if you are joined
By many, many others
With their new attitudes
And their new identities too?
Is it possible
To create a much better world?

'Oh no!'
Says that old familiar little voice
Deep inside your head
'That's a step too far!'

But what if it is possible?
To dream an impossible dream
That then really happens.

One thing is for sure
If you don't believe it can happen
It won't.
Life is about dreaming
And believing
That a much better world
Is just around the corner.

Hierarchy

Hierarchies empower
And disempower
Usually not in equal measure.

All well and good
For those empowered
But not so
For the disempowered.

To be empowered
At the cost of others
Is unhealthy for society.
So why are we
All indoctrinated
To believe
We must have a hierarchy
To thrive?

Intentions or Goals?

Intentions are not goals.
They are though
The more important.

Goals are about
Reaching a point in the future
And are attempts
To direct our future
Believing that we know
What it should be.

So, goals are set by the mind
And, as such, will always be limited.
They are specific
And must be achieved
In order to be successful.
They will require strategy
Plans and some sort of measure
To ensure that each moment
They are being kept on track.
They must also be seen
At this point in time
To actually be achievable…

An intention acts from the moment it's set
It is not only a future destination.
It can be much, much more ambitious
As it does not require knowledge
Right here and now
Of how or when it will be achieved.

It simply requires a willingness
To take one step at a time
Where decisions and choices
Made in the moment
Are the things that are guided
By the intention that's set.

Ambitious intentions
Might be seen by the cynical
As being pie-in-the-sky fantasies
And just figments of imagination.

So, an intention requires
An acceptance of not knowing
How or when it might be achieved.
It requires trust and belief
And absence of doubt.
It requires an open mind
Willing to see signs
And to be ready to follow
The route that calls
Until even the impossible becomes possible!

It is doubt, distrust
And disbelief
That undermines intentions.
So, think positively
And hold those intentions
As you watch for the signs
And follow the guidance…

Easy to Believe

It is so easy to believe
That we as individuals
Cannot bring about
Big changes.
It is how we exonerate
Ourselves
From being responsible
For making any effort!

But what if big changes
Only come about
By the coalescence
Of everyone's small efforts?
Are you at risk
Of joining those on the sidelines
Lamenting because
Things never seem to change?

Perhaps there
There is food for thought…

'As if'

To turn your life around
By starting to live 'As if'
Now that's a really tricky one
But very well worth a try!

To live as if
Your best life has arrived
Your wildest dreams
Have materialised.
Your doubts and fears
Have melted away
And there is joy
To be had every day!

To imagine exactly
How you would feel
If all of that came to pass…
Then to act in a way
As if it is all true…
Can that really be so hard?!

So, Where Might All This Take Us?

Or, at least, where is all this taking me?

You Could Say I Lost a Lot!

Life is not working
It's really not working
I'm so, so exhausted.
It's long overdue the time to move on!

But life is comfortable
I have status and money.
It may feel like a treadmill
Because I have no control
But surely it's better to be a prince not a pauper
Wouldn't you say?

And where would I go?
I really don't know.
What would I do?
It's anyone's guess!
With whom would I be?
Is there anyone out there?
How would I do it?
It's so, so scary.
How would I plan it?
I can't do it alone.
Am I brave enough?
I really don't think so …
How our mind keeps us stuck
When our heart says to go.

But when it comes to the point
That nothing could be worse
Than current existence enduring
It requires a complete and utter leap of faith
No real plans and no guarantees being possible.
But what if I end up with nothing
Or, at least, less than I've got?
See how the mind keeps blocking the way.
By all means plan what you can
But be prepared to lose what you've got.
It's not what you really want anyway!
Eventually, a different life will settle
It just requires one step at a time.

But you will need to dig deep
To fight for yourself
And take on many new challenges.
But these challenges
Are ones you are choosing for yourself
To shift your life forwards
To make your life better.

And if you are poorer
And have much less status
Remember you will also be free.
And that is, believe me, a far greater gift.

It makes you richer than the wealthiest person.
It makes you happier than the wealthiest person.
It certainly makes you more free
Than the wealthiest person
Who is owned by their possessions
And is never really free.

A life without a focus on money and status
Is a life that is quite different you see.
I do say *different* not *worse*
Because I found that that difference was better for me.

But how will *you* know
If you never give it a go?

Manifesto for Change

You can set an intention
For big changes to happen
But it's impossible
To make a plan.
Why?
Because the intended outcome
Needs to be
So very different
From what is familiar now.
And making plans ahead of time
Requires we are familiar with
The sorts of changes required.

But for change to be big
It must be novel
Which means it is essentially
Completely unfamiliar.
So, the method of getting there
Must be unfamiliar too
It needs to be unfettered
In order to be free
To develop exactly as it will.

So, if we really want
Big changes to happen
We must let go
Of the need to plan and control.

This can be very hard to do
At least for the mind
For the ego
It won't even want to go there!

To move beyond
The outdated rules
Big changes need to happen.
So, belief is essential
As is trust and patience
An unswerving conviction
Determination and a lack of fear
About venturing into the unknown.
All together with
An ability to ignore
Any ridicule from those who fear
Such big and novel changes.

Such qualities
Are the things
In which
A new identity needs to believe
So that those new identities
With their new attitudes
And the courage of their convictions
Can nurture
A completely new and unfamiliar
World Order into being.

About the Author

I have a vision of an equitable world where the value of the feminine is equitable to that of the masculine. They are not the same, but their contributions are equitable and, most importantly, synchronistic.

In my trilogy of books, I start with a change of attitude as this is needed before anything else is possible. A new attitude allows for a new identity, the subject of the second book. It is in this final book that I address my ambition of a whole new life which, when joined up with many other new lives, has the potential to shift the inertia that has gripped this world for so long and left it in the hands of the unadulterated masculines, who, though worthy, are not the masters of all the necessary skills.

The feminine has been invalidated for too long and the world suffers as a result. I am not advocating for a dominant feminine as, ultimately, that would create its own set of problems. I am advocating for equity and this is the theme of the trilogy.

My focus has been the feminine. I do not wish to lessen the value of masculines, neither do I wish to live without them! But I do require respect that allows for my life, as a feminine, to be equitable.

Acknowledgements

This page is insufficient to fit all the acknowledgements I would need to make if I were to define even one person specifically.

Suffice to say, if you know me personally, then thank you for your contribution to my life. Every contribution is invaluable and all my connections have shaped me and helped me to become who I am: a happy and confident person (most of the time!).

Index

A Formula   14
All Rolled up Into One   58
A Much Better World   122
An Image   54
'As if'   130
Bamboozled   75
Banishment   106
Beauty   57
Be It!   65
Belief   98
Believers   85
Beyond the Consensus   84
Big, Small or Infinitesimal   112
Boundaries or Barriers?   76
Breathe   24
Busy, Busy   102
Contagion   78
Damaged Ego   70
Disruption   48
Easily Done   38
Easy to Believe   129
Evolving   22
Fallible   99
Fearless   94
First Love   100
Focus   87

Gaining or Losing?   86
Going Forwards   13
Heart Truths   33
Hierarchy   125
House Room   93
I Don't Know   80
If I Were You…   43
If Truth Were Told   46
Illusions   107
Inconvenient Truth   119
Intentions or Goals?   126
Jigsaw   118
Knowing   68
Listening to Our Hearts   39
Living Space   77
Losing Control   16
Love Is the Key!   114
Manifesto for Change   138
Mind-Boggling   26
Mini-Men   82
More Than Enough   42
Must I Really?   18
My Way…   69
Naysayers   60
Ours   34
Pandering   40
Parallel World   116
Pep Talk   62
Persuaded   20
Pyrrhic Victory   88

Rationing   96
Rejects and Misfits   67
Right or Wrong?   45
Right up to the End   17
Selective or Equal?   105
Shadow Side   97
Spotlight   66
Success!   89
The Devil You Know   27
The Line   44
The Meaning of Safe   19
'There'   28
TINA   36
Unconditional Love   120
Unfathomable   104
Who Are We?   53
Wildest Dreams   111
You Could Say I Lost a Lot!   135

www.ingramcontent.com/pod-product-compliance
Lightning Source LLC
Chambersburg PA
CBHW060611080526
44585CB00013B/785